wild and beautiful

GRAND TETON

NATIONAL PARK

photography by FRED PFLUGHOFT *and* HENRY H. HOLDSWORTH

American & World Geographic Publishing / Montana Magazine

Above: Sun rises on the Tetons and Moulton Barn,
on Mormon Row. HENRY H. HOLDSWORTH

Facing page: Aspens in autumn dress. FRED PFLUGHOFT

Title page: The peaks for which the national park is named,
framed by a window. FRED PFLUGHOFT

Front cover: Grand Teton at sunrise from Schwabacher Landing.
HENRY H. HOLDSWORTH

Front cover (flap): Monkeyflowers add magenta to grassy plots
throughout the Teton Range. HENRY H. HOLDSWORTH

Back cover: A grove of aspen screens a view of Oxbow Bend on the
Snake River. FRED PFLUGHOFT

ISBN: 1-56037-153-6
Photography © 2000 Fred Pflughoft, Henry H. Holdsworth,
John L. Hinderman and Jim K. Gores
© 2000 American & World Geographic Publishing
This book may not be reproduced in whole or in part by any means
(with the exception of short quotes for the purpose of review) without
the permission of the publisher. For more information on our books call
or write: American & World Geographic Publishing,
P.O. Box 5630, Helena, Montana 59601,
(406) 443-2842 or (800) 654-1105
www.montanamagazine.com
merle_guy@lee.net

Printed in China

Foreword

Few places in the continental United States offer more dramatic and impressive vistas than Grand Teton National Park. With twelve peaks rising a mile or more above the valley floor of Jackson Hole, these mountains known collectively as the Tetons are the hub of one of the most photographed places in North America.

With that in mind, I set out to capture on film the essence of this grand place. I knew I had to include all of the standard, favorite and best views of the Tetons, but I also wanted to include some views that not everyone sees.

Wildlife that makes this part of Wyoming their home is also an important part of the story. Henry, a superb landscape photographer, also has a keen eye for photographing wildlife in its environment.

The resulting portfolio of images shows off the grandness both large and small of this special place. We hope that, as you move through these pages, each image presents its own beauty, but also summons memories of your own time in the Tetons. Whether you came as a tourist, a climber or hiker who challenged the many peaks or trails, one of the countless photographers who visit each year, or one of those fortunate few who live and work at the foot of this magnificent range, we believe we have offered something that will remind you of why you think this place is so grand.

So, come along and enjoy your travels through this wild and beautiful place.

—*Fred Pflughoft*

An immature northern harrier in the grass of Jackson Hole.
HENRY H. HOLDSWORTH

Left: From a storm cloud, a rainbow touches down near
Mount Moran. HENRY H. HOLDSWORTH

Corner of an old barn on Mormon Row, and the Teton peaks. FRED PFLUGHOFT

Facing page: Water, frozen atop the Tetons and flowing below. FRED PFLUGHOFT

Sunshine on shoulder of Mount Moran and Jackson Lake, from Signal Mountain. FRED PFLUGHOFT

Mount Moran, reflected in String Lake. FRED PFLUGHOFT

Cow moose, lunching in lilies. HENRY H. HOLDSWORTH

Clouds move in on the Teton peaks. FRED PFLUGHOFT

Facing page: Beneath frosted cottonwoods, Ditch Creek remains fluid on a sub-zero morning. HENRY H. HOLDSWORTH

At home on the range; a Jackson Hole bison herd, up with the sun. HENRY H. HOLDSWORTH

Great gray owl perches above sticky geraniums. HENRY H. HOLDSWORTH

Right: Hedrick Pond reflects the Tetons at sunrise.
HENRY H. HOLDSWORTH

A deep-winter frost hovers above a bison and below the snowy Teton peaks. HENRY H. HOLDSWORTH

Facing page: View of the Tetons from Oxbow Bend, a quiet meander of the Snake River. FRED PFLUGHOFT

White pelican shopping for lunch. HENRY H. HOLDSWORTH

Left: A breezy afternoon on Jenny Lake. FRED PFLUGHOFT

The Cathedral view of the Tetons looms above the Old Patriarch, a twisted pine. FRED PFLUGHOFT

A driving, late spring snow turns the head of a mule deer doe. HENRY H. HOLDSWORTH

Following pages: In late spring, the sun sets over Jackson Lake. FRED PFLUGHOFT

Past their peak of brilliance, the leaves of aspen fade to orange. FRED PFLUGHOFT

Facing page: Big rock, little rock—the Tetons reflected in Jenny Lake. FRED PFLUGHOFT

Following pages: The Snake River in shadow and the Tetons in light of the rising sun. FRED PFLUGHOFT

Chapel of the Transfiguration in the national park, blessed with a view of the Tetons, welcomes worshippers. FRED PFLUGHOFT

Right: Aspen trunks, with backs turned to the autumn sunlight.
FRED PFLUGHOFT

Below: A male sage grouse spreads his tail feathers in a courtship
dance. HENRY H. HOLDSWORTH

Migrating elk herd heads toward the National Elk Refuge at the southern end of the park.

HENRY H. HOLDSWORTH

Mount Moran holds snow in its couloirs on a sunny autumn day, looking from Oxbow Bend. FRED PFLUGHOFT

Right: A western tanager perches as leaves emerge.
HENRY H. HOLDSWORTH

Below: Indian paintbrush adds to a grassy palette in Grand Teton National Park. HENRY H. HOLDSWORTH

As snow falls, Canada geese take flight. HENRY H. HOLDSWORTH

Facing page: Cascade Creek plunges over Hidden Falls. FRED PFLUGHOFT

Above: A family of bald eagles above the
Snake River. The new member is a week old.
HENRY H. HOLDSWORTH

Right: Lupine proliferates in the meadows of
Grand Teton National Park. HENRY H. HOLDSWORTH

Paddling across String Lake with Mount Moran looming on the far shore. FRED PFLUGHOFT

Following pages: Sun silhouettes the Tetons and reflects the scene on the surface of Oxbow Bend. FRED PFLUGHOFT

The Cathedral view of the Teton peaks, reflected in String Lake. FRED PFLUGHOFT

A sandhill crane escorts its young colt through the grass along the Buffalo River.
HENRY H. HOLDSWORTH

A grove of aspen screens a view of Oxbow Bend on the Snake River. FRED PFLUGHOFT

With snows lingering on the Tetons, boats at Jackson Lake's Colter Bay Marina are ready for cruising. FRED PFLUGHOFT

At sunrise, a bull moose crosses
a shallows in Oxbow Bend.
HENRY H. HOLDSWORTH

Sagebrush flourishes in the flats below the Tetons. FRED PFLUGHOFT

Spider project spans stems of grass and catches the light of the sun.
JIM K. GORES

Looking across Jenny Lake to the mouth of Cascade Canyon.
FRED PFLUGHOFT

Climber and belayer, in concert, on the Grand Teton. FRED PFLUGHOFT

Clouds partially obscure a view of the Tetons from Jackson Lake. FRED PFLUGHOFT

Left: A river otter treads on crusty ice.
HENRY H. HOLDSWORTH

Below: Mount Owen holds pockets of snow in the warm months. FRED PFLUGHOFT

Facing page: Snow coats the ground, fence and cottonwoods on a sub-freezing morning. FRED PFLUGHOFT

The Tetons, trees and autumn alpenglow reflect
in the Snake River, from Schwabacher Landing.
JOHN L. HINDERMAN

Left: Moisture, in several forms and layers, graces a spring landscape. HENRY H. HOLDSWORTH

Below: A male mountain bluebird perches at the top of a pine. HENRY H. HOLDSWORTH

Sagebrush, aspens and the snowy peaks of the Tetons in autumn. FRED PFLUGHOFT

Right: Mount Moran, as seen through a window of Jackson Lake Lodge. FRED PFLUGHOFT

Below: Like a Scandinavian fell, a low hill separates a cross-country skier from the Teton peaks. FRED PFLUGHOFT

Following pages: Sunrise with clouds over Jackson Lake, from Signal Mountain. FRED PFLUGHOFT

Lake Solitude separates a shoreline rock from the Grand Teton peaks. FRED PFLUGHOFT

A trumpeter swan and Rocky Mountain, or yellow, pondlilies, which Native Americans called *woka*. HENRY H. HOLDSWORTH

A coyote and a yellow wildflower lift their heads above ground cover. HENRY H. HOLDSWORTH

Left: The Tetons, shrouded in a thunderstorm at sunset. HENRY H. HOLDSWORTH

A backpacker heads up the Cascade Canyon trail. FRED PFLUGHOFT

Sunrise at Jackson Lake. FRED PFLUGHOFT

Alpenglow warms an old barn along Antelope Flats Road and the Tetons. JOHN L. HINDERMAN

Branches and Teton peaks, covered with snow. FRED PFLUGHOFT

Autumn huckleberry, with Mount Moran reflected on the surface of String Lake. FRED PFLUGHOFT

Autumn sun illuminates aspen leaves. FRED PFLUGHOFT

Left: Winter landscape near the Moose entrance to Grand Teton National Park. FRED PFLUGHOFT

A great blue heron lifts off the water. HENRY H. HOLDSWORTH

Facing page: Rising sun on Grand Teton. HENRY H. HOLDSWORTH

Arrowleaf balsamroot, also called mule ears.
JIM K. GORES

Snowfields on granite—Mount Teewinot at sunrise. HENRY H. HOLDSWORTH

Bull elk in an icy mist on the National Elk Refuge. HENRY H. HOLDSWORTH

A black bear, up to his snout in huckleberry bushes. HENRY H. HOLDSWORTH

Facing page: Mount Moran, reflected on the placid surface of String Lake.
FRED PFLUGHOFT

Following pages: The Teton Range in the light of late autumn. FRED PFLUGHOFT

Above: A juvenile common merganser conquers turbulent waters.
FRED PFLUGHOFT

Right: The Old Patriarch Tree and the Tetons. HENRY H. HOLDSWORTH

Snow falls on a cow and bull moose near Oxbow Bend. HENRY H. HOLDSWORTH

Aspens stand leafless and tall in winter. HENRY H. HOLDSWORTH

A pair of trumpeter swans, as if choreographed. HENRY H. HOLDSWORTH

Right: Oxbow Bend, with mist hovering at sunrise. FRED PFLUGHOFT

Left: Golden-leaved aspens brighten Jackson Hole in autumn. FRED PFLUGHOFT

Below: Canada goose goslings less than an hour old, hover around their mother on the National Elk Refuge. HENRY H. HOLDSWORTH

Early autumn at the outlet of Jenny Lake, near Teewinot Mountain. FRED PFLUGHOFT

Right: Moose, silhouetted by sunrise at Oxbow Bend.
JOHN L. HINDERMAN

Below: Winter is on its way. FRED PFLUGHOFT

Sticky geranium graces Grand Teton National Park. HENRY H. HOLDSWORTH

Facing page: A patch of open water holds out against winter as the sun fades behind the Tetons. FRED PFLUGHOFT

Oblivious to what looms behind them, white pelicans bathe in sunlight on Oxbow Bend of the Snake River. HENRY H. HOLDSWORTH

Falling waters and mosses on Cascade Creek. FRED PFLUGHOFT

Weathered fence, weathered barn and weathered rock. FRED PFLUGHOFT

Above: A Uinta ground squirrel scratches an itch. FRED PFLUGHOFT

Left: Wyoming chiaroscuro: The Tetons from Schwabacher Landing.
FRED PFLUGHOFT

Below: A beautiful butterfly, streamside. FRED PFLUGHOFT

Mount Teewinot, viewed from the Moose Ponds. FRED PFLUGHOFT

Dark clouds settle over the Tetons at dawn. HENRY H. HOLDSWORTH

Sunrise shines a spotlight on aspens at Oxbow Bend and leaves Mount Moran in shadows. HENRY H. HOLDSWORTH

Rising sun casts its light on Tetons, while Snake River and its valley wait to be warmed. HENRY H. HOLDSWORTH

An ermine emerges to survey a winter scene. HENRY H. HOLDSWORTH

Facing page: Sun sets on the Tetons, with Lake Solitude in shadow.
FRED PFLUGHOFT

Water tumbles over rocks on creek flowing into Jenny Lake. FRED PFLUGHOFT

A burst of balsamroot in Grand Teton National Park. FRED PFLUGHOFT

Left: Mount Moran shines at sunrise amidst all the colors of a rainbow.
HENRY H. HOLDSWORTH

Below: Wildflowers flank the steady steps of a stream. HENRY H. HOLDSWORTH

Faded aspen leaves are backed by coniferous green. FRED PFLUGHOFT

Left: White pelicans form a line before a cow moose in Oxbow Bend. HENRY H. HOLDSWORTH

Right: Tetons upon Tetons. FRED PFLUGHOFT

Below: Fringed gentian blooms among leaves of grass.
HENRY H. HOLDSWORTH